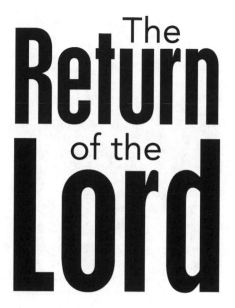

The Return of the Lord

A Bible Prophecy Overview
Plus Significant Details

Clyde J. Zehr

WESTBOW
PRESS®
A DIVISION OF THOMAS NELSON
& ZONDERVAN

WestBow Press books may be ordered through booksellers or by contacting:

WestBow Press
A Division of Thomas Nelson & Zondervan
1663 Liberty Drive
Bloomington, IN 47403
www.westbowpress.com
844-714-3454

ISBN: 978-1-6642-0101-9 (sc)
ISBN: 978-1-6642-0100-2 (e)

Library of Congress Control Number: 2020914497

Print information available on the last page.

WestBow Press rev. date: 12/01/2020

PREFACE

When telling about events to occur on earth at the time of His glorious coming again, Jesus said: *"Now when these things begin to happen; look up and lift up your heads, because your redemption draws near." Then He spoke to them a parable. "Look at the fig tree, and all the trees. When they are already budding, you see and know that summer is now near. So you also, when you see these things happening, know that the Kingdom of God is near. Assuredly, I say to you, this generation will by no means pass away till all things take place. Heaven and earth will pass away, but My words will by no means pass away."* (Luke 21:28-33 NKJV).

Immediately following these remarks, our Lord told three more parables, explaining what He meant by the instruction for us to look up and lift up our heads. Those parables are a call to watchfulness, faithfulness, and fruitfulness.

Profoundly, we are the generation that will witness the prophesied end time events occurring. Each and every effort, therefore, to further assist the followers of Jesus Christ in responding to His exhortation to be watchful, faithful, and fruitful to the very end should be gratefully received and seriously considered.

INTRODUCTION

During the first week of January, 2018, I received in the mail a New Year's greeting from Carol, my sister-in-law. After her well wishes for the coming year, she asked simply: *What is your "take" on the end times?* I was as eager to respond to her request as I was curious regarding what her request actually was. Carol is a faithful, dedicated Christian. She is familiar with the many biblical prophecies concerning things to come. It seemed to me that she was asking, given the occasion of the beginning of a new year, for a timely scriptural update. In other words: *What's up?* In my mind I re-phrased her question to read: *Clyde, prophetically speaking, is anything going to happen in 2018 that I should be aware of?*

Actually, possibly so. The next prophetic event to occur on earth could indeed have taken place in 2018. God is proceeding according to the divine chronological plan He has had in mind from the beginning. That plan, righteous in nature and revealed to us in Scripture, indicates that human history is heading toward a climactic period of events. The timing of these coming events is in His hands, but current world conditions would warrant the next prediction taking place now, or in the immediate future. True, things could get worse, but they certainly seem bad enough already to necessitate God's sovereign intervention.

A meaningful reply to Carol's implied question would include two efforts. One would be to examine the Bible's description of the next world-impacting event to occur. The other would be to place that event in the context of the scriptural *big picture* of the last days. With such an overview in mind of God's glorious plan to transition from the Church Age to the Kingdom Age, we would then be able to say as much as could be said about 2018, and beyond.

My response to Carol's request was a series of letters mailed over an extended number of months. With her permission, those letters are now the chapters of this book. When writing each letter, my desire was, by the Lord's enabling, to be as much a source of encouragement as information. That is still my desire.

CJZ
June, 2020

DEDICATION

To
Leona

CONTENTS

Preface v

Introduction vii

Dedication ix

Chapter 1   Where Are We Now? 1

Chapter 2   The Reason for Our Lord's Return 6

Chapter 3   The Millennial Kingdom of God 12

Chapter 4   Daniel's Seventieth Seven 16

Chapter 5   The Great Tribulation 21

Chapter 6   The Wrath of God 27

Chapter 7   The Ingathering of the Redeemed 34

About the Author 39

CHAPTER ONE
Where Are We Now?

Dear Carol,   January 2018

Greetings. Explaining my "take" on the end times will take some time. When God brings to a close an era of human history, He sovereignly does many things, to put it mildly. Graciously, our Heavenly Father has given us a prophetic big picture of all that is about to happen. Equally significant, He has, in advance, revealed specific world events which we are to anticipate and watch for.

According to Scripture, God is getting ready to make a change in the way He does things around here. Ours is the generation that will experience this historic, divinely-initiated change as it unfolds. This is the biggest thing about us! Two thousand years ago, our risen Lord's great commission to His church was to go throughout the entire world with the good news of the gospel. He concluded by saying: *And surely I am with you always, to the very end of the age* (Matthew 28:20 NIV). The *end of the age* does not refer to the end of the world, or of the human race, but rather to the end of the Church Age! There is still more to come. God's master plan for the redemption of mankind is not over yet. However, the Church Age will give way to the Kingdom Age. Soon, saving grace will be proclaimed throughout the world during a glorious 1000-year period in which Jesus will reign as King of the earth from His throne in Jerusalem.

Having said this, let's begin with a simple, straight-forward question: prophetically, where are we now? This is easy. Our generation is in the time period between the last biblical prophecy that took place on the face of the earth and the next one that is to occur. The point to notice is that this time period, having extended now for about 70 years, is ending. The next prophetic event could well occur in 2018, or perhaps in 2019, maybe a few years after that. Prophetically speaking: *soon, at the door.*

You no doubt recall the last actual prophetic event to happen on earth. That was when the Jewish people, after almost 2000 years of being exiled from the Holy Land, established the state of Israel. Incredible! And yet, few events have been more frequently prophesied in Scripture.

> *When all these blessings and curses I have set before you come upon you and you take them to heart wherever the Lord your God disperses you among the nations... then the Lord your God will restore your fortunes and have compassion on you and gather you again from all the nations where he scattered you. Even if you have been banished to the most distant land under the heavens, from there the Lord your God will gather you and bring you back. He will bring you back to the land that belonged to your fathers, and you will take possession of it. He will make you more prosperous and numerous than your fathers.* (Deuteronomy 30:1-5 NIV).

You can also look at Isaiah 11:10-12; Amos 9:11-15; Ezekiel 37:1-14, 20-28; Jeremiah 31:7-14, 31-40; Jeremiah 33:6-16; Zechariah 10:6-12. I could send you another list of Bible references equally as long. Clearly, in the wisdom and sovereign will of God,

His gracious redemptive program for the sons and daughters of Adam includes the actual, historical re-establishing of the nation of Israel at the close of the Church Age.

Even after all these years we still look back in utter amazement at what took place. People of Jewish descent have returned to the land that God gave to Abraham! The nation of Israel has been re-born! On May 14, 1948, in the city of Haifa, Jewish statesmen officially declared the state of Israel as an independent sovereign nation among the nations of the world. Then, on June 7, 1967, Israel's military forces captured East Jerusalem, with the result that the unified city of Jerusalem became the nation's capital.

Before going on, I will just mention that, as predicted, Jewish people have for now returned to the Holy Land in unbelief. They are indeed the children of Abraham, but sadly, they do not know the God of Abraham.

Since 1948 a multitude of what we might call pre-prophecy events have occurred in the Middle East. Who can keep track of them all? None of these seemingly endless conflicts and wars is predicted in the Bible. However, there can be no doubt that they are setting the stage for the next prophetic event to take place as God now transitions to the Kingdom Age.

The next biblical prophecy to occur is perhaps not so generally well known. Ten countries around the Mediterranean Sea will form a 10-nation coalition for political, economic, and military unity. Egypt, Libya, and Ethiopia are actually listed in Scripture by name (Daniel 11:43). For now, we don't know for certain which other seven countries will be included. You can take a map of the area and work your way around the Mediterranean Sea, giving thought to possible combinations of nations.

This 10-nation coalition, which I am calling the Mediterranean Union or MU, will rule the Mediterranean world with an iron fist. American and Russian influence will be greatly limited as the MU will be fully committed to controlling its' own neighborhood.

If this 10-nation coalition does not come into existence, then you don't have to bother yourself by listening to me anymore. But then, of course, it will! Beginning in the second chapter of Daniel and extending through Scripture, predictions are given about these *ten kings who have not yet received a kingdom, but who for one hour* (that is- a short time) *will receive authority as kings along with the beast. They have one purpose and will give their power and authority to the beast* (Revelation 17:12 NIV). The prophet, Daniel, in his customary condensed manner, predicted simply: *In the time of those kings, the God of heaven will set up a kingdom that will never be destroyed* (Daniel 2:44 NIV).

All we need is for the upheavals in the Middle East (that is, the chaos, the wars, the displacement of millions of people, and other forms of widespread human suffering) to motivate ten leaders, and the people of ten countries, to say: E*nough is enough. The Mediterranean world is our home. Let's join forces and take control of our lives.* God, who is really in control, has His own timetable. Humanly speaking, however, the chaos in the Middle East certainly seems sufficient for the MU to form this year. We will see.

Plainly stated, the prophetic significance of the formation of the MU will be its' gradual, but greatly intensifying, negative impact on the nation of Israel. While not a member of the 10-nation coalition, Israel will, almost overnight, find itself geographically located in the middle of a newly-formed regional world power with which it will have to deal.

I need to pause and make clear that I am talking about actual events that take place in specific geographical locations. As you know, the Bible is filled with prophetic insights regarding the dire conditions on earth in the end times. Truth will be thrown to the ground (Daniel 8:12, 2 Thessalonians 2:10-11), wickedness will increase (Matthew 24:12), scoffers will come, ridiculing the very truths we are discussing (2 Peter 3:3), false prophets will appear and deceive many (Matthew 24:11), ignorance of the Bible will be widespread (Amos 8:11-13), lawlessness will abound (2 Thessalonians 2:6-7), and more. Yes, I know. This is heavy. Later, we will certainly need to consider more closely this worldwide moral collapse.

One dominant point, with regard to an overview of actual events, is that once the MU coalition is established, additional end time predictions will begin occurring in rapid succession, one after another, overlapping each other, right up to the day of our Lord's return to earth. This is the meaning of Daniel's words: *The end will come like a flood* (Daniel 9:26 NIV). In other words, all prophesied events of the last days are in abeyance until the MU is formed. This one specific scriptural prediction needs to take place before a groundswell of related prophecies can occur. Students of the Bible will need to have their prophetic big picture well in place then.

Granted, 70 years is a long time period between one fulfilled prophecy and the next, and people can tend to lose concentration. Be that as it may, we need to begin preparing ourselves for the reality that such lengthy periods separating fulfilled prophecies are forever ending.

This is our first step in obtaining an overview of the last days. Next time we will consider the biblical reason for Jesus' return. I am quite surprised that more is not being said about this. The purpose of our Lord's return is so stunningly profound, and precious almost beyond comprehension, that we can hardly stand before it at all. We are mentally and emotionally subdued. In humility, we offer up the final prayer in the Bible- *Amen. Come, Lord Jesus* (Revelation 22:20 NIV).

I will close with words spoken by the Lord Jesus that pertain specifically to us: *Now when these things begin to happen, look up and lift up your heads, because your redemption draws near...When you see these things happening, know that the kingdom of God is near. Assuredly, I say to you, this generation will by no means pass away till all these things take place. Heaven and earth will pass away, but My words will by no means pass away* (Luke 21:28, 31-33 NKJV).

Yours, in Christ,
Clyde

CHAPTER TWO

The Reason for Our Lord's Return

Dear Carol,   March, 2018

As you no doubt recall, on the Mount of Olives at the very moment of our Lord's ascension, angels said to the disciples: *Men of Galilee... why do you stand here looking into the sky? This same Jesus, who has been taken from you into heaven, will come back in the same way you have seen him go into heaven* (Acts 1:11 NIV). Days prior to that, when informing the disciples of His soon departure, Jesus said: *Do not let your hearts be troubled...I will come back and take you to be with me* (John 14:1, 3 (NIV). Later, the disciples asked Him: *Tell us...when will this happen, and what will be the sign of your coming and the end of the age* (Matthew 24:3 NIV)?

Ever since these words were spoken, each generation of the church has anticipated this *blessed hope- the glorious appearing of our great God and Savior, Jesus Christ* (Titus 2:13 NIV). Throughout the history of the church, Christians have lived with the expectation that Jesus would return in their lifetime. His not returning as they anticipated does not take away from their sincere desire to be found faithful when He arrived.

Why is Jesus coming again? This, beyond all contradiction, is the big question to be answered in our quest for the scriptural overview of things to come. The answer to this question is profound!

The full and comprehensive reason for our Lord's return can be summarized this way: *in order for God's gracious program for the redemption of fallen mankind to be continued to consummation, Jesus Christ must return to earth, and He will.* As we examine this reason, our focus will be on the words, *continued to consummation.*

Lets' begin, then, with the fundamental reality that this old world is not going to last forever. More to the point, God's offer of salvation will not last forever either. There is a consummation to God's vast, historic work of granting new life in Christ. A date is set. God's loving offer of redeeming grace for Adam's fallen race will come to a conclusion. An end will occur.

The Bible tells us when this consummation will take place. Revelation chapters 20 and 21 reveal that this divine work of the redemption of mankind will continue until that final generation of the coming 1000-year Kingdom of God on earth. Then, and only then, will God's offer of atonement through Christ reach completion. Then, and only then, will this present heaven and earth be destroyed by fire, and the new heaven and new earth of the eternal order come into being. Then God will have lifted the human race back to what it was designed to be.

There is a final day. Until the final hour of that final day, God presses on with His glorious redemptive work. Everything that God does is anchored in the reality that He *is longsuffering toward us, not willing that any should perish but that all should come to repentance* (2 Peter 3:9 NKJV). Human beings are highly created, richly endowed, and deeply fallen. And yet each person, loved by God, can be restored. The blood of Jesus Christ goes as far a sin has gone. No one is beyond the reach of God's atoning grace. Generations come and go, and yet each generation bears spiritual fruit. Someone has so beautifully said: *There is not a dull page in all this age-long story of the redeeming of the human race.*

However (and this is certainly one gigantic "however"), during mankind's time on earth there are four generations in which the continuation of God's saving grace is placed in peril. On four occasions the powers of evil are so arrayed against a specific generation that, if not checked, pose a serious threat to this divine work of grace extending to the following generation. Four times Satan deceives earth's population into mounting such a titanic, worldwide, collective rebellion against the God of the Bible that would, apart from divine intervention, prevent the continuation to the consummation of God's plan for man's redemption.

Specifically, these four generations are those living on earth at the time of Noah (Genesis chapters 6-9), those living on earth at the time of the Tower of Babel (Genesis 11:1-9), our generation at the close of the Church Age (II Timothy 3:1-5), and that final generation living at the close of the coming 1000-year Kingdom Age (Revelation 20:1-10). The similarity of these four generations is that, in each, the saints of God find it extremely difficult, if not impossible (God knows!), to pass the message of salvation in Christ Jesus on to the generation to follow.

Fortunately, God is never caught off guard. When things look perilous, hopeless and impossible, when evil men have done their worst, then God reveals His remarkable solutions. In each of these four crisis generations He **reverses things** by sovereignly intervening in human affairs, bringing to pass a unique, once only, never to be repeated, world-changing event. Our Lord's glorious return to earth is one of these four events.

We remember from our early Bible study days that the maintaining of the human race in a savable state is one of the unconditional benefits of the cross of Jesus Christ. From Genesis chapter three onward, the Holy Spirit has supernaturally undergirded humanity, preventing our collectively descending to such a devil-inspired level of wickedness and self-worship that we could not comprehend the divine offer of redemption, nor make a personal response to it. Whether or not we have been consciously aware of this ongoing work of the Holy Spirit, He deserves our praise for such a comprehensive expression of divine love. Yet, on these four occasions, for God's work of redemption in Christ Jesus to continue, a unique intervention of sovereign grace becomes necessary.

We certainly don't need to be reminded that the words of the Apostle Paul remain true: *Now we see but a poor reflection as in a mirror...now I know in part* (1 Corinthians 13:12 NIV). Be that as it may, because we know God, there are four affirmations that we can boldly make with complete confidence.

First, God flooding the whole earth, destroying the wicked, while preserving Noah and his family, was not just the best way, but it was the **only** way to maintain the human race in a savable condition.

Second, God shattering the arrogant unity at Babel by separating the population of the earth into language groups, and then scattering those groups to form the nations of the world, was not just the best way, it was the **only** way to reverse mankind's self-deification and keep them savable.

Third, God sending His Son Jesus, King of Kings and Lord of Lords, to gather unto Himself His church, pour out holy wrath on the ungodly, and then begin His reign over the nations of the world from His throne in Jerusalem, is not just the best way, but it is the **only** way to stem the present global rebellion, maintain our ability to respond to the gospel, and insure that multitudes will be saved in the Kingdom Age as redeeming grace continues.

Fourth, God sovereignly deciding, at the close of the Kingdom Age, to extend no longer *the day of salvation* (2 Corinthians 6:2 NIV), but rather to bring His work of redeeming grace to its' glorious consummation, is caught up in the mystery of divine wisdom, justice, and love.

Our generation is being called upon in Christ to recognize conditions worldwide as they actually are. This is the challenge before us. The Apostle Paul's prophetic summary can be a good starting point: *But mark this: There will be terrible times in the last days. People will be lovers of themselves, lovers of money, boastful, proud, abusive, disobedient to their parents, ungrateful, unholy, without love, unforgiving, slanderous, without self-control, brutal, not lovers of the good, treacherous, rash, conceited, lovers of pleasure rather than lovers of God* (2 Timothy 3:1-4 NIV).

We might add to the list intolerant, lack of civility, insisting that God be marginalized out of every aspect of daily human activity, ignorant of the value of the human soul, and totally blind to the crisis that mankind is facing. This is a description of a generation that is removed about as far as possible from the life God would have us to live. We are unique living beings. We have been created in God' image. Our purpose, and privilege, is to love God and enjoy fellowship with Him forever. The prophetic picture before us is of people who have lost whatever values and virtues they once had that prevented them from pandering to their pagan, self-centered, and prideful instincts.

No wonder the people of God have been so caught off guard! In no way were we anticipating anything like this. The devil's present onslaught against the human race is of an intensity scarcely seen before. Rarely (only twice before) has such a coordinated, worldwide, demon-inspired, anti-God rebellion occurred.

The people described by the Apostle Paul have one common characteristic. They insist on having the last word. They themselves must have the final say on how they behave, or don't behave; what they choose to believe, or choose not to believe; what their duty is to God and those around them, if any. Not having a fixed point of reference by which to determine truth, shame, reason, or the meaning of life is proving to be ruinous for them. The future belongs to those who allow God to have the last word. More than allow! We rejoice in our Creator having the final word, because He is the only One who can get it right. From the very beginning it was never intended that we should make it on our own.

This level of cosmic rebellion can only be reversed be Almighty God sovereignly intervening in human affairs. As twice before, mankind can only be maintained in a savable state by a divinely initiated, never before experienced, global event. Jesus Christ, rending the eastern sky, coming in majesty, accompanied by thousands times ten thousand angels, will do it. *At that time the sign of the Son of Man will appear in the sky, and all the nations of the earth will mourn. They will see the Son of Man coming on the clouds of the sky, with power and great glory* (Matthew 24:30 NIV).

There have been many great saints who have appeared on the pages of human history. This present dark time will bring greatness out of many more.

Next, we will have the joy and delight of looking at what the Bible says concerning the 1000-year Kingdom that Jesus will establish when He comes. My goodness! It will be almost heaven!

Yours, in the shelter of the Most High,
Clyde

CHAPTER THREE

The Millennial Kingdom of God

Dear Carol,   July, 2018

Peace to you, and joy, in the Lord. We now turn our attention to the glorious 1000-year Kingdom that our Lord, when He returns, will establish on the earth. There is a plan, that plan is centered in Christ Jesus, and that plan will work. In answer to our prayers, God's Kingdom comes!

Jesus Christ will **personally** (1 Thessalonians 4:16), **visibly** (Revelation 1:7), **locally** (Zechariah 14:4), **triumphantly** (Matthew 24:30), and **bodily** (Matthew 25:31) return to planet earth. Our Lord's return will be followed by His 1000-year reign (Revelation 20:6) as king over all nations (Zechariah 14:9) from His throne in Jerusalem (Zechariah 8:3). The Jewish people will be redeemed (Deuteronomy 4:30, Isaiah 51:11, Hosea 3:5), regathered to the land of Israel (Ezekiel 36:24-38), and have a phenomenal ministry in assisting the nations of the world to worship and obey their God and King (Exodus 19:5-6, Isaiah 61:6, Ezekiel 37:24-28, Zechariah 8:23).

Just because Jesus will rule over all the nations of the world from His throne in Jerusalem does not mean that all people on earth are saved. It means that Jesus will **rule** from His throne, and all nations must obey His whether they want to or not, for He will rule them with a rod of iron (Psalm 2:9, Revelation 12:5). Obedience will be strictly enforced (Zechariah 14:16-19).Satan will be bound, and demonic activity will be non-existent (Revelation 20:1-3).

All people on earth will come before Jesus **as nations** (Isaiah 2:2-3; Zechariah 2:10-13, 8:20-22; Psalm 2:7-10, 72:8-11). Each nation, on a regular schedule, will send a delegation to Jerusalem, bearing gifts, to worship their King and receive His instructions to insure that justice, righteousness, and peace will prevail throughout the earth. Best of all, *the earth will be filled with the knowledge of the glory of the Lord, as waters cover the sea* (Habakkuk 2:14 NKJV).

This sounds glorious, and glorious it will be! There will be no more war. Disputes between nations and people groups will be a thing of the past (Isaiah 2:4). Fierce animals will be tamed (Isaiah 11:6-9).The ground will become remarkably fertile (Amos 9:13-15). Every conceivable aspect of daily life on earth will be good. Throughout a time period of one thousand years the inhabitants of the earth will enjoy **ever increasing global good**.

However (and this is certainly one gigantic "however"), the main purpose of our Lord's return to earth is to continue to consummation the divine plan of redemption. The idea is not that people should be wonderfully blessed here on earth, but then left unprepared for eternity. The Lord is going to use this temporal global good to motivate individuals to become aware of their spiritual need. He will lead them to consider their baffling reluctance to be humbly thankful for the remarkable peace and blessings of daily life, and their puzzling inability to wholeheartedly worship Him as God. By comparison, currently in the Church Age, God opens the eyes of serious seekers to their spiritually-dead condition by graciously enabling them to realize that they cannot overcome **evil** in their own strength. In the Kingdom Age, serious seekers will become aware of their spiritually-dead condition by being graciously enabled to realize that they, in themselves, are unable to appropriately respond to **good**. Those hungering for reality will be told something like this: *You can't wholeheartedly worship and obey Christ, nor rejoice in His goodness, because you do not have the spirit to do so. You are* *spiritually dead. When your father, Adam, left the Garden of Eden he was physically alive but spiritually dead. As his descendant, that is your condition.* Therefore, as marvelous as it is for you to have the Son of God reigning in Jerusalem as King of all nations, you must have Him in your heart as the Savior and Lord of your life. The message of the cross will be given. Multitudes, in numbers that we cannot even imagine, will respond by faith to God's saving grace.

The Bible reveals that, at the end of the glorious 1000-year Kingdom Age, Satan will be released and the restraint on evil will be briefly lifted (Revelation 20:7). Incomprehensibly, a rebellion by devil-deceived nations will take place that almost overwhelms the saints (Revelation 20:8-9). But Christ triumphs (Revelation 20:9-10), God's redemptive plan for the human race reaches its' glorious consummation, this present world is destroyed by fire, and the new heaven and new earth of the eternal order come into being (Revelation 20:11-22:6).

There is no way to not be greatly impressed by the sheer number and clarity of prophetic statements in the Bible about this coming Kingdom. Three are included here.

Zechariah 2:10-13 (NIV): *Shout and be glad, O Daughter of Zion. For I am coming, and will live among you, declares the Lord. Many nations will be joined to the Lord in that day and will become my people. I will live among you and you will know that the Lord Almighty has sent me to you. The Lord will inherit Judah as His portion in the holy land, and again will choose Jerusalem. Be still before the Lord, all mankind, because he has roused himself from his holy dwelling.*

Zechariah 14:4, 9, 16-19 (NIV) *On that day his feet will stand on the Mount of Olives, east of Jerusalem, and the Mount of Olives will be split in two from east to west, forming a great valley, with half of the mountain moving north and half moving south…The Lord will be king over the whole earth. On that day there will be one Lord, and his name the only name…Then the survivors from all the nations that have attacked Jerusalem will go up year after year to worship the King, the Lord Almighty, and to celebrate the Feast of Tabernacles. If any of the people of the earth do not go up to Jerusalem to worship the King, the Lord Almighty, they will have no rain. If the Egyptian people do not go up and take part, they will have no rain. The Lord will bring on them the plague he inflicts on the nations that do not go up to celebrate the Feast of Tabernacles. This will be the punishment of Egypt and the punishment of all the nations that do not go up to celebrate the Feast of Tabernacles.*

Isaiah 2:2-4, 17-18 (NIV): *In the last days the mountain of the Lord's temple will be established as the chief among the mountains; it will be raised above all the hills, and all nations will stream to it. Many people will come and say, 'Come, let us go up to the mountain of the Lord, to the house of the God of Jacob. He will teach us his ways, so that we may walk in his paths.' The law will go out from Zion, the word of the Lord from Jerusalem. He will judge between the nations and will settle disputes for many peoples. They will beat their swords into plowshares and their spears into pruning hooks. Nation will not take up sword against nation, nor will they train for war anymore...The arrogance of man will be brought low and the pride of man humbled; the Lord alone will be exalted in that day, and the idols will totally disappear.*

And more! Equally amazing are Isaiah 9:7, 11:1-10, 12:4-6, 35:1-10; Jeremiah 3:17, 23:1-8; Daniel 2:44-45, 7:27; Zechariah 8:3, 20-22; Psalm 2:7-10, 47:7-9, 72:8-11, 102:15-18; Revelation 20:1-6.

There will be a seven-year transition period between the present Church Age and this coming Kingdom Age. I have known all along that the time would come when we would need to set everything else aside, and turn our attention completely to this transition period. My next letter, and all future letters, will focus on these prophecies that will so profoundly touch our lives.

Be still, and know that I am God; I will be exalted among the nations, I will be exalted in the earth (Psalm 46:10 NIV).

Yours, in Him,
Clyde

CHAPTER FOUR
Daniel's Seventieth Seven

Dear Carol,   October, 2018

Let us not give up meeting together, as some are in the habit of doing,
but let us encourage one another- and all the more as you see the Day
approaching (Hebrews 10:25 NIV). I call your attention to those
final words- *as you see the Day approaching.* The writer of the book
of Hebrews so beautifully takes this for granted. Rightly so, since
a call to watch for the Bridegroom's arrival (Mathew 25:1-13) is so
central in our instructions from the Lord. The challenge, however,
is to watch in keeping with Scripture. The Bible makes it clear that
seeing the day of our Lord's return approaching involves also the
observing of a climatic seven-year time period drawing near.

We are told that the events associated with the second coming
of Christ, and the close of the New Testament era, will not happen
all at once. Rather, the convergence of those many predictions will
take place over a period of exactly seven years. We are informed that
there is going to be a significant seven-year transition between the
Church Age which is familiar to us, and the Kingdom Age which
we find joy in anticipating but see dimly. The Bible describes in
chronological order, and in incredible detail, events to transpire
during these coming seven years.

For us, of course, this is more than academic research! We are the generation that will not only see these events approaching, but will experience them taking place. A day is soon coming when this seven-year transition will begin. We will be here when that day arrives. On one specific day this prophetic countdown will commence. We will witness that commencement taking place.

Let me pause to call attention to one key fact which we will at another time consider much more in detail, that is, when the seven years will begin! This approaching transition will begin on the very day that the nation of Israel and a soon to be formed ten-nation Mediterranean coalition sign an interim seven-year peace treaty. I mention this briefly now to emphasize that this starting day that we are to watch for will be seeable, hearable, and knowable. It will make the news. We will be fully aware that it has occurred.

While attempting to avoid the extremes of being unduly technical or unhelpfully brief, the fact is that a working knowledge of this era-concluding transition begins in the Old Testament book of Daniel. There we are told that the coming seven-year period is, in reality, Daniel's seventieth *seven*, a time period within the great prophet's profound prediction recorded in chapter nine. In response to Daniel's prayer, God sent the angel, Gabriel, who revealed to him not only a remarkable but a truly indispensable chronological time frame of things to come. *Seventy 'sevens' are decreed for your people and your holy city to finish transgression, to put an end to sin, to atone for wickedness, to bring in everlasting righteousness, to seal up vision and prophecy and to anoint the most holy. Know and understand this: From the issuing of the decree to restore and rebuild Jerusalem until the Anointed One, the ruler, comes, there will be seven 'sevens' and sixty-two 'sevens'. It will be rebuilt with streets and a trench, but in times of trouble. After the sixty-two 'sevens,' the Anointed One will be cut off and will have nothing. The people of the ruler who will come will destroy the city and the sanctuary. The end will come like a flood: War will continue until the end, and desolations have been decreed. He* (that is, the antichrist person) *will confirm a covenant with many for one 'seven.' In the middle of the 'seven' he will put an end to sacrifice and offering. And on the wing of the temple he will set up an abomination that causes desolation, until the end that is decreed is poured out on him* (Daniel 9:24-27 NIV).

Seventy 'sevens' are decreed (vs. 24). Briefly, Gabriel informed Daniel that a certain specific timeframe of seventy seven-year periods must take place before Jesus triumphantly returns as King of the earth. The first of those seven-year periods would begin on the very day that Nehemiah received official permission from the Persian King, Artaxerxes, to return to Israel and rebuild the city of Jerusalem (see Nehemiah 2:1-8). The final seven-year period in the series would conclude on the day in which our Lord, at the close of the Church Age, returns to earth, coming in judgment, and standing once again on the Mount of Olives near Jerusalem (see Zechariah 14:4, 9).

Sixty-nine groups of Daniel's seventy seven-year periods, each following immediately after the previous one, have long since passed into history. The sixty-ninth period ended on the day of our Lord's triumphant entrance into Jerusalem on Palm Sunday. That is to say, 483 of the 490 prophetic years came to a conclusion on that most noteworthy day. But then, and equally noteworthy, Gabriel revealed to Daniel that two event would occur **after** the close of the sixty-ninth seven but **before** the beginning of the seventieth-seven (that is, the crucifixion of our Lord in 32 AD, and the destruction of the city of Jerusalem in 70 AD) establishing the significant fact that the seventieth *seven* would not begin immediately after the close of the sixty-ninth *seven*. Saying this in another way, Gabriel spoke to Daniel regarding 490 prophetic years, not 490 consecutive years. True, the first 483 years were consecutive, but not the final 7 years. There is an unspecified time gap between the final two seven-year periods. Over 1900 years have come and gone, and that final seven-year period has not yet taken place. It remains to be fulfilled.

We are living in the time span between the sixty-ninth and seventieth seven-year periods of Daniel's prophecy. Actually, we will be the last who will do so. This lengthy time period, known biblically as the *times of the Gentiles* (Luke 21:24 NIV), is none other than the glorious New Testament Church Age, which is drawing to a close.

Our Lord's words have echoed down the corroders of time for over nineteen centuries, stirring the hearts of His saints generation after generation: *I am sending you to them* (that is, all people everywhere) *to open their eyes and turn them from darkness to light, and from the power of Satan to God, so that they may receive forgiveness of sins and a place among those who are sanctified by faith in me* (Acts 26:17-18 NIV). May our efforts have been worthy of His Name.

Things now change! The long awaited seventieth *seven* begins. We are told in advance what to expect. Whether or not Daniel, first of all, and then other prophetic writers to follow, had any idea there would be such a large gap of time until their words were fulfilled, they certainly were given to know the characteristics of those transitional years when they arrived. In our immediate future things will steadily go from bad to worse. As the global, demon-inspired rebellion against God intensifies, secular humanism will permeate every aspect of society. According to Scripture, faithfully living a godly life in Christ Jesus will become increasingly challenging.

I am enclosing a diagram of Daniel's seventieth *seven*. Having something visual to refer to will be helpful as we consider the chronological framework of the transition period we see approaching. God has given us a clear picture of where human history is headed, what to anticipate, and how to maintain a strong witness for Christ as the New Testament era draws to a close. As you can see in the diagram, the seven-year transition is divided into three smaller time periods: *the beginning of birth pains, the great tribulation,* and *the wrath of God.*

Next time, after briefly considering *the beginning of birth pains,* we will seek to get our minds informed and our emotions sorted out regarding the second time division, *the great tribulation.* We are told that, within the coming transition, there will be a short, exceptionally dark, period of persecution. The Bible reveals what this actually will be, who will be affected, and how long it will last.

Yours, in Christ,
Clyde

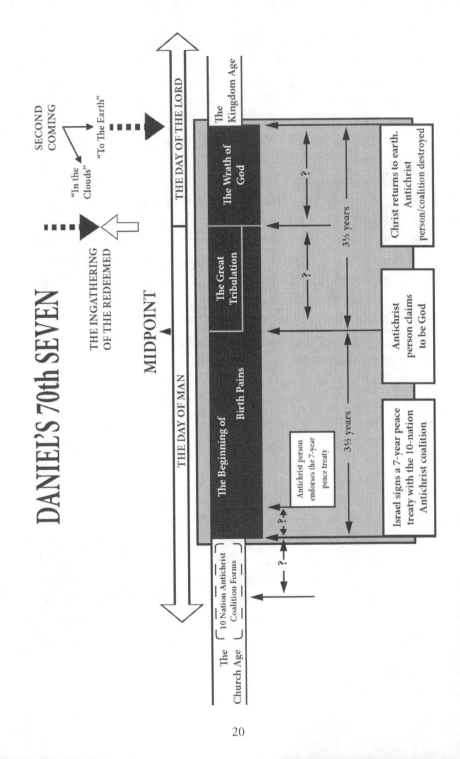

DANIEL'S 70th SEVEN

SECOND COMING

"In the Clouds"

"To The Earth"

THE INGATHERING OF THE REDEEMED

MIDPOINT

THE DAY OF THE LORD

THE DAY OF MAN

The Church Age

10 Nation Antichrist Coalition Forms

The Beginning of Birth Pains

The Great Tribulation

The Wrath of God

The Kingdom Age

Antichrist person endorses the 7-year peace treaty

3½ years

3½ years

3½ years

Israel signs a 7-year peace treaty with the 10-nation Antichrist coalition

Antichrist person claims to be God

Christ returns to earth. Antichrist person/coalition destroyed

CHAPTER FIVE

The Great Tribulation

Dear Carol,   January, 2019

Greetings in the Name of Him with Whom all things are possible.

And you will be hearing of wars and rumors of wars; see that you are not frightened, for those things must take place, but that is not yet the end. For nation will rise against nation, and kingdom against kingdom, and in various places there will be famines and earthquakes. But all these things are merely the beginning of birth pangs. Then they will deliver you up to tribulation, and will kill you, and you will be hated by all nations on account of My name...but he who endures to the end will be saved...Therefore when you see the ABOMINATION OF DESOLATION which was spoken of through Daniel the prophet standing in the holy place...then there will be a great tribulation, such as has not occurred since the beginning of the world until now, nor ever shall be. And unless those days had been cut short, no life would have been saved; but for the sake of the elect those days shall be cut short (Matthew 24:6-9, 13, 21-22 NASB).

As you are well aware, the overall picture given us of the days ahead is a grim one. We are told of ever increasing levels of spiritual deception, God-denying secular humanism, loss of personal freedom, global devastation, and eventually, divine judgment. That is certainly dark! Mankind's unrepentant spiritual decline is even reflected in the names of the three biblical subdivisions of the coming seven-year period. With slight variations in wording in different English translations of the Bible, they are the *beginning of birth pains* (Matthew 24:8 NIV), *great tribulation* (Matthew 24:21 NASB), and *wrath of God* (Romans 5:9 NASB). Each of these three is different in the actual years and months it will occupy in the overall transition period, although there will be some overlapping. They also differ as to those who will suffer in each subdivision, and the reason why they will be afflicted.

We will look briefly at the beginning of birth pains and then consider more in detail the great tribulation. In seeking to do this we find ourselves introduced to a quite unique feature of biblical prophecy itself. We are to primarily obtain an understanding of worldwide developments during the seventieth *seven* <u>by being informed about the specific events</u> that will occur as the nation of Israel relates to the coming 10-nation Mediterranean coalition. The Bible gives few details regarding actual forms of spiritual deception and secular humanism that will manifest themselves worldwide. Rather, we are to understand that whatever is prophesied to take place in the Mediterranean region will, in a similar manner, occur in all nations. Therefore, to be specifically informed of events as they develop in that one geographical region of the world is to be informed, in general, of events occurring globally.

Especially helpful is the fact that specific dates that we really want to know about are revealed to us through happenings that will take place in the Mediterranean world. For example, as we prepare ourselves for the seven-year transition from the church era to the kingdom era, we can't help wondering about the actual date when that transition will start. What does the Bible say? The scriptural answer is that things begin on the day in which the nation of Israel establishes a significant formal relationship with the 10-nation coalition. The angel, Gabriel, revealed to Daniel that the countdown begins the day that Israel signs a seven-year interim peace agreement with that newly formed regional coalition (Daniel 9:27). On that very day the seventieth *seven* begins, not just in the Mediterranean area, but worldwide. Another example, which we will examine in this letter, is that on the specific day when the deception in that "peace" treaty is finally exposed, the great tribulation will begin, in Jerusalem, the Mediterranean region, and around the world.

Let me pause to reflect that I have at times referred to the coming 10-nation coalition as "the Mediterranean Union." I will now move beyond that designation, using instead "the 10-nation antichrist coalition," as this more clearly expresses its' true nature. There will be both an antichrist system as well as an antichrist person. *The ten horns you saw are ten kings who have not yet received a kingdom, but who for one hour* (that is- a short time) *will receive authority as kings along with the beast* (the antichrist person). *They have one purpose and will give their power and authority to the beast. They will make war against the Lamb, but the Lamb will overcome them because he is Lord of lords and King of kings* (Revelation 17:12-14 NIV).

Now we look briefly at the first of the three subdivisions of the seventieth *seven*, the one that is identified as the beginning of birth pains. The first day of the seven-year transition period will also be the first day of these afflictions. We read that a staggering increase in human suffering and death will take place. The reason given is that the instances of all too familiar, but tragic, events such as wars, famine, disease, and earthquakes, will intensify worldwide (see Revelation 6:1-8). For the most part, people caused to suffer by these calamities will be, as always has been, those who happen to be in harm's way.

One overarching word that describes this period of birth pains is the term, "intensify." We are not to anticipate anything particularly new or unique. Rather, human difficulties unfortunately familiar to us will increase. Chaos and confusion will result in the increase and intensifying of national regimes of dictatorial rule. There is an old saying that if people must choose between chaos and tyranny, they will choose tyranny. Personal freedoms will increasingly be restricted. Related to that, instances of the intolerance we now see directed by some toward others who they consider to be "politically/religiously incorrect" will multiply. One deception that will particularly intensify is the idea that all problems facing mankind can be resolved without divine help. This will result in the manifesting of the glory of man's own strength and the exaltation of the human spirit. Have I mentioned recently that the human race is highly created, richly endowed, and deeply fallen?

At some point, as these birth pains proceed, an additional persecution, quite cruel in nature, will commence that will be systematic, official, and extremely selective; so much so that our Lord said there had never been a time like this before (Matthew 24:21). Influenced by Satan, the nations of the world will enact governmental regulations that are blatantly anti-God. Those who refuse to comply with these rules will be viewed as problematic, narrow, disloyal, and opponents of a new world order. They will be singled out for severe persecution, even elimination. This dark period is called the great tribulation.

In Matthew 24:9-29 our Lord gave us an overview of the great tribulation (see also Mark 13:9-23 and Luke 21:12-24). Immediately following His description of the beginning of birth pains (Matthew 24:6-8), He transitioned by saying: *Then you will be handed over to be persecuted and put to death, and you will be hated by all nations because of me...but he who stands firm to the end will be saved* (Matthew 24:9, 13 NIV). Significantly, while in the process of revealing the stressfulness for all of us during this singularly difficult time, Jesus turned His full attention specifically to the distress to take place in the city of Jerusalem. In doing that He identified the starting date of the great tribulation, not just in that city but worldwide. Our Lord referred to a persecution that would **begin** with the desecration of the Jewish temple. *Therefore when you see the 'abomination of desolation,' spoken of by Daniel the prophet, standing in the holy place... then there will be great tribulation, such as has not been since the beginning of the world until this time, no, nor ever shall be* (Matthew 24:15, 21 NKJV). But notice! The abomination that makes desolate will occur in **the exact middle** of Daniel's seventieth *seven. He* (the antichrist person) *will confirm a covenant with many for one 'seven.' But in the middle of the 'seven' he will put an end to sacrifice and offering. And on the wing of the temple he will set up an abomination that causes desolation* (Daniel 9:27 NIV). That the great tribulation will begin at the exact midpoint of Daniel's seventieth seven-year period is a foundational biblical certainty.

The Hebrew phrase that is translated into English as *the abomination of desolation* is a historical expression that has a singular meaning. It is used in the Bible to refer to two identical blasphemous events, one that occurred in the second century BC, and the other is yet to take place. These are the two times in which a false idol is erected in, of all places, the temple of God in Jerusalem, behind the veil, in the holy of holies, that one sacred place reserved for the presence of Almighty God, the Creator of heaven and earth.

In 168 BC Antiochus Epiphanes, a Syrian king, marched his army into Jerusalem and causes the Jewish sacrificial system of worship to cease. He had his soldiers carry a statue of Zeus, his chief god, into the holy of holies, and demanded that the Jewish people worship that image (see Daniel 11:29-32). Chaos erupted that lasted three years. The final result was a divine deliverance. Jewish freedom fighters were enabled to drive the mighty Syrian army out of Israel, arrange a peace accord with Antiochus, and cleanse and rededicate the temple to the Lord.

The second *abomination of desolation* will take place when the antichrist person (a forceful, charismatic, and popular official representing the 10-nation antichrist coalition) has a picture or statue of himself paraded into the most holy place in a newly-built Jewish temple, and demands that he be worshipped as God. We are told that this *man of lawlessness...will oppose and will exalt himself over everything that is called God or is worshipped, so that he sets himself up in God's temple, proclaiming himself to be God* (2 Thessalonians 2:3-4 NIV). On that very day he will become the supreme ruler of the antichrist coalition of nations. Beginning on that specific day, to be "religiously/politically correct" in the Mediterranean world, people will be required to worship this antichrist person, and receive his mark on their right hand or forehead (see Revelation chapter 13).

Continuing with the chronology of events, Jesus then taught us about the duration of the great tribulation. He said: *If those days had not been cut short, no one would survive, but for the sake of the elect those days will be shortened* (Matthew 24:22 NIV). If this period of distress is not shortened, it could theoretically last exactly three and one-half years, that is, until the end of Daniel's seventieth *seven,* and our Lord's glorious return. Mercifully, however, it will not last that long! This period of unprecedented selective persecution will begin at the midpoint of the seven-year transition period, but will not continue until the end of that period. On a day determined by, and known only to, God Himself, it will be cut short.

After describing the persecution to occur in Jerusalem, our Lord ended His teaching regarding the great tribulation with a statement that is worldwide in scope: *At that time if anyone says to you, 'Look, here is the Christ!' or, 'There he is!' do not believe it. For false Christs and false prophets will appear and perform great signs and miracles to deceive even the elect- if that were possible. See, I have told you ahead of time. So if anyone tells you, 'There he is, out in the desert,' do not go out; or, 'Here he is, in the inner room,' do not believe it* (Matthew 24:23-26 NIV). The Lord's clear indication is that, just as will occur in the 10-nation antichrist system, so throughout all regions of the world, self-deifying imposters will appear, perform miracles, and demand allegiance.

In the next letter, with glory and praise to the Almighty, we will review the Scriptures describing the coming just and righteous punishment to be poured out on the wicked, called the wrath of God.

Triumphantly in Christ,
Clyde

CHAPTER 6

The Wrath of God

Dear Carol,   April, 2019

Greetings. We continue in our desire to obtain a clear biblical overview of our Lord's soon return. Our confidence that He is sovereignly in control of all that is going to take place will be strengthened even more as we give our attention to an event which we have suspected all along would happen sometime, that is, the wrath of God.

There is a basic principle of divine government that all things, both the good and the evil, must reach ripeness (see Genesis 15:16 and 18:16-33). Therefore, as man's willful spiritual rebellion against God progresses through Daniel's predicted seventieth *seven,* wickedness will increase and things will go from bad to worse as human evil ripens toward divine punishment. We now know it is not because the world is not Christian enough that our Lord has not yet come, but rather that the world is not wicked enough.

Ripeness will occur (Revelation 14:17-19)! Only God Himself will know when that moment will have arrived (Matthew 24:36). When that time does indeed come, the very nature and character of God demand that He judge this sinful world for its iniquity. That's all there is to it! Our Sovereign Lord Himself will personally unleash this wrath upon sinners. In His own words: *Vengence is Mine. I*

WILL REPAY, says the Lord (Romans 12:19 NASB). Significantly, the entire world will be fully aware that these calamities are the vengeance of God, not an attack by some hostile government or a random act of nature (Revelation 6:17). The writer of the book of Hebrews couldn't have said it better: *It is a terrifying thing to fall into the hands of the living God* (Hebrews 10:31 NASB).

I pause to observe that this happens to be the very first time that our thoughts are directed toward a coming end time event which has nothing to do with us personally. The Bible vividly describes this coming judgment, predictions which we will faithfully examine, although we ourselves will simply not be involved. *God did not appoint us to suffer wrath, but to receive salvation through our Lord Jesus Christ* (1 Thessalonians 5:9 NIV). *Much more then, having now been justified by His blood, we shall be saved from the wrath of God through Him* (Romans 5:9 NASB). We need to remind ourselves that God is calling us *to wait for his Son from heaven- Jesus, who rescues us from the coming wrath* (1 Thessalonians 1:10 NIV). In the next letter we will enjoy the wonderful Scriptures which describe that divine rescue, that glad day!

Plainly stated, the coming wrath will be a brief outpouring of divine punishment on an exceptionally wicked generation living on earth. This will not be the end of the world, nor is it the destruction of mankind. There is still much more to come in God's gracious plan for the redemption of the human race. For now, however, the first thing our Lord will do when He returns is to unleash a righteous, but limited, outburst of His fury on all those who have participated in the demon-influenced, global rebellion against Him. The punishment will fit the crime!

Scripture refers to this future divine judgement as both the day of the Lord and as the wrath of God. We read: *Alas for the day! For the day of the Lord is near, and it will come as destruction from the Almighty...The day of the Lord is indeed great and very awesome, and who can endure it?* (Joel 1:5, 2:11 NASB). We also read: A*nd the kings of the earth and the great men and the commanders and the rich and* *the strong and every slave and free man, hid themselves in the caves and among the rocks of the mountains; and they said to the mountains and the rocks, 'Fall on us and hide us from the presence of Him who sits on the throne, and from the wrath of the Lamb; for the great day of their wrath has come; and who is able to stand?'* (Revelation 6:15-17 NASB).

Some terms need to be defined. To begin, we want to distinguish the day of man from the day of the Lord. The day of man is that time starting with Adam's disobedience until the second coming of Christ when sinful men and women have liberty, under the permissive will of God, to do what they please. In fact, the great tribulation will be the final chapter in the day of man. The day of the Lord begins with the return of Christ in the clouds. His visible presence in power and great glory will bring an end to the day of man. From that moment on, people will no longer be permitted to do just as they please (see Psalm 2:7-12; Zachariah 14:16-19; and Revelation 9:6). Once started, the day of the Lord will continue until the final consummation, with the ushering in of the new heavens and the new earth of the eternal order (see Revelation 21:1-4).

There is also a need to understand the relationship between the day of the Lord and the wrath of God, terms which are used interchangeably in Bible prophecy. Again, the day of the Lord is none other than that time when Jesus is personally, visibly, locally, bodily and triumphantly here with us, first in the clouds and then on the earth. Not only here with us, but never to leave us again! The day of the Lord, which will encompass innumerable events and activities throughout the 1000-year Kingdom Age, will begin with a brief outpouring of divine punishment on the wicked that is called the wrath of God. Therefore both of these time segments, the coming wrath and the coming millennial Kingdom, are parts of the larger day of the Lord.

We are informed that, while punishment of the wicked will be administered by the Lord Himself, the specific acts of vengeance will be executed by avenging angels. Each and every one of the seven trumpet judgments, including hailstorms and locusts

(Revelation 8:1- 9:21), and each and every one of the seven bowl judgments, including painful sores and rivers turned to blood (Revelation 16:1-21) will be inflicted on earth by angels sent from heaven. We are reminded of the Bible's description of God's judgment upon Egypt: *He unleashed against them his anger, his wrath; indignation and hostility- a band of destroying angels* (Psalm 78:49 NIV). In a similar manner, the Apostle Paul boldly declared: *God is just: He will pay back trouble to those who trouble you and give relief to you who are troubled...This will happen when the Lord Jesus is revealed from heaven in blazing fire with his powerful angels. He will punish those who do not know God and do not obey the gospel of our Lord Jesus* (2 Thessalonians 1:6-8 NIV).

Most significantly, we are told that a dramatic sign will be given to indicate that this divine punishment is about begin- namely, cosmic disturbances in the heavens. Joel prophesied: *The sun will be turned to darkness and the moon to blood before the coming of the great and dreadful day of the Lord* (2:31 NIV). Isaiah wrote: *The stars of heaven and their constellations will not show their light, The rising sun will be darkened and the moon will not give its light...I will make the heavens tremble; and the earth will shake from its place at the wrath of the Lord Almighty, in the day of his burning anger* (13:10, 13 NIV). In Revelation John declared: *I watched as he opened the sixth seal. There was a great earthquake. The sun turned black like sackcloth made of goat hair, and the whole moon turned blood red, and the stars in the sky fell to earth, as late figs drop from a fig tree* (6:12-13 NIV). Then, our Lord Himself said: *Immediately after the tribulation of those days the sun will be darkened, and the moon will not give its light; the stars will fall from heaven, and the powers of the heavens will be shaken. Then the sign of the Son of Man will appear in heaven, and then all the tribes of the earth will mourn, and they will see the Son of Man coming on the clouds of heaven, with power and great glory* (Matthew 24:29-30 NKJV).

The symbolic language in these verses is quite apparent, and one wonders as to just what exactly is being predicted. Regardless, we can say with certainty that there will be the appearance of cosmic disturbances associated with the beginning of the wrath of God. But notice- the appearance of these disturbances will occur **before** that judgment begins (Joel 2:31), and **after** the great tribulation (Matthew 24:29)! See the enclosed diagram.

The unmistakable nature of this coming divine wrath is clearly revealed in what turns out to be a surprisingly large number of prophetic biblical descriptions of this punishment to come. In addition to three passages listed here, see also Isaiah 13:6-13; Joel 1:15, 2:1-2, 10-11, 30-31, and 3:14-16; Amos 5:18-20; Revelation 14:17-19.

Isaiah 2:12, 17-21 (KJV): *For the day of the Lord of host shall be upon every one who is proud and lofty, and upon every one who is lifted up, and he shall be brought low…And the loftiness of man shall be bowed down, and the haughtiness of man shall be made low; and the Lord alone shall be exalted in that day. And the idols he shall utterly abolish. And they shall go in to the caves of the rocks, and into the holes of the earth. In that day a man shall cast his idols of silver, and his idols of gold, which they made each for himself to worship, to the moles and to the bats; To go into the clefts of the rocks, and into the tops of the ragged rocks, for the fear of the Lord and for the glory of his majesty, when he arises to shake terribly the earth.*

Zephaniah 1:14-18 (NKJV): *The great day of the Lord is near; It is near and hastens quickly. The noise of the day of the Lord is bitter; There the mighty men shall cry out. That day is a day of wrath, a day of trouble and distress, a day of devastation and desolation, a day of darkness and gloominess, a day of clouds and thick darkness, a day of trumpet and alarm against the fortified cities and against the high towers. I will bring distress upon men, and they shall walk like blind men, because they have sinned against the Lord; Their blood shall be poured out like dust, and their flesh like refuse. Neither their silver nor their gold shall be able to deliver them in the day of the Lord's wrath; But the whole land shall be devoured by the fire of His jealousy. For He will make a speedy riddance of all those who dwell in the land.*

1 Thessalonians 5:2-3 (NASB): *For you yourselves know full well that the day of the Lord will come just like a thief in the night. While they are saying, 'Peace and safety!' then destruction will come upon them suddenly like birth pangs upon a woman with child, and they shall not escape.*

Next time we will turn our attention to the assuring biblical teaching that the church will not be present on earth when all this takes place. Believers in Christ Jesus need not be concerned about this brief, but severe, divine punishment as it occurs worldwide because they will have been **raptured** already.

Looking up,
Clyde

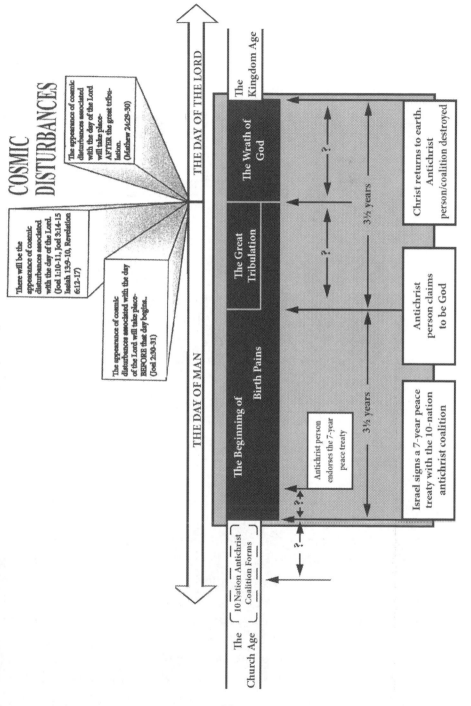

COSMIC DISTURBANCES

There will be the appearance of cosmic disturbances associated with the day of the Lord. (Joel 1:10-11, Joel 3:14-15 Isaiah 13:9-10, Revelation 6:12-17)

The appearance of cosmic disturbances associated with the day of the Lord will take place AFTER the great tribulation. (Matthew 24:29-30)

The appearance of cosmic disturbances associated with the day of the Lord will take place BEFORE that day begins. (Joel 2:30-31)

THE DAY OF MAN

THE DAY OF THE LORD

The Church Age

10 Nation Antichrist Coalition Forms

The Beginning of Birth Pains

The Great Tribulation

The Wrath of God

The Kingdom Age

Antichrist person endorses the 7-year peace treaty

3½ years

3½ years

?

?

?

?

Israel signs a 7-year peace treaty with the 10-nation antichrist coalition

Antichrist person claims to be God

Christ returns to earth. Antichrist person/coalition destroyed

33

CHAPTER SEVEN
The Ingathering of the Redeemed

Greetings Carol,   July, 2019

Listen, I tell you a mystery: We will not all sleep, but we will all be changed- in a flash, in the twinkling of an eye, at the last trumpet. For the trumpet will sound, the dead will be raised imperishable, and we will be changed (1 Corinthians 15:51-52 NIV).

According to the Lord's own word, we tell you that we who are still alive, who are left till the coming of the Lord, will certainly not precede those who have fallen asleep. For the Lord himself will come down from heaven, with a loud command, with the voice of the archangel and with the trumpet call of God, and the dead in Christ will rise first. After that, we who are still alive and are left will be caught up together with them in the clouds to meet the Lord in the air. And so we will be with the Lord forever. (1 Thessalonians 4:15-17 NIV).

Our Lord's coming one glad day to gather us unto Himself is more than a doctrine, it is a living hope. The Apostle Paul proclaimed that all believers, in their generation, are to *live self-controlled, upright, and godly lives in this present age, while we wait for the blessed hope, the glorious appearing of our great God and Savior, Jesus Christ* (Titus 2:12-13 NIV). This is that singular hope which, throughout the ages, has enabled the people of God to persevere no matter how difficult the circumstances of their lives might have been. Little wonder that the final prayer in the Bible is: *Amen. Come, Lord Jesus* (Revelation 22:20 NASB).

Given our deep personal desire, longing, and anticipation of finally seeing the Lord Jesus face to face, there is a possibility that we may fail to take note of what He who controls the entire universe by His almighty power is saying to us. Plainly stated, that coming glad day will be the grand and glorious ingathering of the redeemed. With the notable end time exception of 144,000 descendants of Abraham (Revelation 7:1-7, 14:1-5), this is that day, that instant, in which Jesus Christ will finally, for the first time, gather before Himself each and every soul who believes in Him. Starting with Genesis chapter four and moving forward, all those who previously died trusting in Jesus will be **resurrected** and taken up to meet the Lord in the air. The following instant all Christians alive on earth at that time will be **raptured** bodily to be united with Christ in the clouds. In the blink of an eye, the **redeemed**, all the saints of all ages, will meet the Lord somewhere above planet earth. At that moment, standing before the Lord in transfigured, glorified bodies, will be His triumphant united church of all time, referred to in Scripture as the bride of Christ (Revelation 19:7-8).

The Bible has much to say about this ingathering of all the saints of all times and all lands at the moment of our Lord's triumphant return. First mentioned are those in Christ who will be raised from the dead. This phenomenal occurrence is none other than the first resurrection! *This is the first resurrection. Blessed and holy is the one who has a part in the first resurrection; over these the second death has no power, but they will be priests of God and of Christ and will reign with Him for a thousand years* (Revelation 20:5-6 NASB). Our Lord referred to this glorious moment as *the resurrection of the righteous* (Luke 14:14 NIV). The point is that **only** the saints will be raised at this time. The rest of the dead do not come to life until the thousand years are ended (Revelation 20:5, 11-15).

Joining the saints resurrected from the dead will be those who are raptured. We are told that *the dead in Christ will rise first. After that, we who are still alive and are left will be caught up together with them in the clouds to meet the Lord in the air. And so we will be with the Lord forever. Therefore encourage each other with these words* (1 Thessalonians 4:16-18 NIV).

The word, rapture, does not itself appear in any verse in the English Bible. Our English word, rapture, comes from the Latin verb, rapere, which means, among other things, to seize hastily, to draw to oneself by a sudden movement. The word is used in the Latin translation of the original Greek word in 1 Thessalonians 4:17 (NIV) where it is declared...*we will be caught up.* Historically, the English word, rapture, while not a scriptural term, has been used extensively to designate the catching away, or transporting, of all living believers to meet the Lord in the air at His second coming.

We now come to the unique way in which prophecy regarding this ingathering of all the saints is presented in Scripture. At times the resurrected saints and the raptured saints are spoken of together as one glorious assembly (Revelation 7:9-17). At other times, those resurrected from the dead are referred to separately by themselves, with no word at all about those alive who will be raptured (Luke 14:14 and 20:35, Philippians 3:11, Revelation 20:5-6). Interestingly, and understandably, by far most of the prophetic references are presented solely from the perspective of those to be raptured, that is, those living on earth but in harm's way because of God's coming wrath, with no accompanying comment whatsoever concerning that incredibly large number of saints who will, almost simultaneously, be raised from the dead. For example-*Two men will be in the field; one will be taken and the other left. Two women will be grinding with a hand mill; one will be taken and the other left* (Matthew 24:40-41 NIV). *Therefore you do not lack any spiritual gift as you eagerly wait for our Lord Jesus Christ to be revealed. He will keep you strong to the end, so that you will be blameless on the day of our Lord Jesus Christ* (1 Corinthians 1:7-8 NIV). *Concerning the coming of our Lord Jesus Christ and our being gathered to Him, we ask you, brothers, not to become easily unsettled or alarmed* (2 Thessalonians 2:1 NIV). *And now, dear children, continue in him, so that when he appears we may be confident and unashamed before him at his coming* (1 John 2:28 NIV).

In a similar manner, when indicating that the ingathering of the redeemed and the beginning of divine wrath being poured out on the wicked will both occur on the same day, our Lord described coming events from the perspective of those alive on earth. Those to be resurrected from the dead are not mentioned at all. He taught that, just as the judgment flood began on the same day, but only after Noah and his family entered the ark (Matthew 24:37-39; Luke 17:26-27), and just as the judgment fire fell from heaven the same day, but not until Lot with his family members were escorted safely out of Sodom (Luke 17:28-30), so will it be with the coming of the Son of Man. God's judgment on the wicked will begin the same day, but only after the righteous are delivered from danger by being raptured. As in the deliverance of both Noah and Lot, it is the divine removal of living saints from a situation of impending judgment that, in effect, initiates that very judgment.

In Revelation chapter seven, this event like no other event is gloriously described as if it had already taken place. *After this I looked and there before me was a great multitude that no one could count from every nation, tribe, people and language, standing before the throne and in front of the Lamb. They were wearing white robes and were holding palm branches in their hands. And they cried out with a loud voice: 'Salvation belongs to our God, who sits on the throne, and to the Lamb.'...Then one of the elders asked me, 'These in white robes- who are they, and where did they come from?' I answered, 'Sir, you know.' And he said, 'These are they who have come out of the great tribulation; they have washed their robes and made them white in blood of the Lamb.* (Revelation 7:9-10, 13-14 NIV). That the resurrected saints are said to come out of the great tribulation simply means that, while in the wisdom and power of God the raising of the dead could take place at any time, He has chosen the final day of that tribulation period for this historic event to occur. For the living saints to be said to come out of the great tribulation simply means that our Heavenly Father did what any loving father would do when his children are in danger.

Little is revealed in Scripture regarding our treasured ongoing experiences with the Lord once we are united with Him in the air. The reason no doubt is that we wouldn't be able, ahead of time, to personally embrace such rapturous realities anyway. However, the little that has been said is just exactly what we want to hear! We will be with our Lord forever (1 Thessalonians 4:17); we will be like Him (1 John 3:2); and we will be granted the privilege, although beyond our capability now to comprehend, of participating with Him in the administration and spiritual ministry of His glorious earthly Kingdom (Revelation 3:21, 20:6).

I am coming quickly; hold fast what you have, in order that no one take your crown...He who has an ear, let him hear what the Spirit says to the churches (Revelation 3:11, 13 NASB).

With confidence in Christ,
Clyde

ABOUT THE AUTHOR

Rev. Clyde J. Zehr is a missionary, Bible teacher, and church administrator whose ordained ministry began in 1963. Organizationally, he served with One Mission Society (formerly the Oriental Missionary Society), International Headquarters in Greenwood, Indiana; the Korea Evangelical Holiness Church, International Headquarters in Seoul, Korea; and the Evangelical Methodist Church, International Headquarters in Indianapolis, Indiana.

A native of Kansas, Rev. Zehr graduated from the University of Kansas in Lawrence, Kansas, with a Bachelor of Science degree. After meeting the Lord and starting things over, he received his Master of Divinity degree from George Fox University in Newberg, Oregon; a Bachelor of Languages degree (Korean) from Yonsei University in Seoul, Korea; and a Master of Business Administration degree from Seattle University in Seattle, Washington.

Throughout his ministry Rev. Zehr has been an avid student of Bible prophecy concerning the last days.

Clyde's wife, Leona, who as he says, *was God's gift to me, the love of my life, my best friend, loving mother of Karen and Mark, my co-worker in ministry, missionary partner in South Korea, and my daily prayer partner for sixty-one precious years,* ascended into the presence of the Lord in July, 2018.

Rev. Zehr is retired, and lives in Seattle.

Printed in the United States
By Bookmasters